We Have To Leave The Earth

i.m. Josephine Butler (1828-1906)
and to my children
Melody, Phoenix, Summer, and Willow
with love

We Have To Leave The Earth

Carolyn Jess-Cooke

Seren is the book imprint of
Poetry Wales Press Ltd.
Suite 6, 4 Derwen Road, Bridgend, Wales, CF31 1LH
www.serenbooks.com
facebook.com/SerenBooks
twitter@SerenBooks

ISBN: 978-1-78172-643-3
ebook: 978-1-78172-644-0

The publisher acknowledges the financial assistance of the Books Council of Wales.

Cover artwork: Thirza Schaap, 'beehive' (2017)

Printed in Bembo by Severn, Gloucester.

Contents

III
The House of Rest

IV

Will you tell us the stories that make us uncomfortable, but not complicit?

Ada Limón, *The Carrying*

Now

Now is the moment I sit in bed on one hip, turned
to the round mirror and the back of our daughter who now
climbs into bed, pulling the covers haphazardly across us and
the dog who snores lightly, his coat fox-red in the lunar
TV light, and I think of how she is to start school
in September, I think of what tomorrow asks and what is yet
to be done and undone, how many nows make up a life
and what is living
if not recognising the value of now, if not
refusing to grasp violently at the trespassing of now into then
and knowing that every now is altered in its remembering
just like the round mirror across from me now holds the bed
and the tussled sheets and the heaped shape of our dog
imperfectly, a not-quite now, translating now in five
senses, an infinite now
in sense and meaning
and thus both impossible and exact – now knows no next,
my daughter sleeps by the dog, and I write of them only
because the folding away of light gives a voice
to what cannot be stilled, to that
which will not be etched
or retained in itself, which is why love is the base principle
of time, at once reflecting and illuminating passages
to their possibility of loss, the unknown,
the empty bed
and yet each now restores love, is made of it.

I

Songs for the Arctic

We too flicker briefly

December. Bone sky.

Ocean's oil-dark

cloth unsettled

by a new burden: boat

skirted with white

mountains of many quarries

and quiffs. We watch for

 green sky-rivers

 arrows of geese

 water-scythes of whales

to subtitle this most

unearthly of earth's

scapes. To reassure

that we too

can pass gently

through

Snow Letters

At Cape North

      three picnic tables

           peeking out of snow

                spalted bright

                    may yet return

Confrontation

Why did you come?

To the serrated wastes, wolf-winter,

flukkra incessant as loneliness,

light pared to a foil.

I think of Amundsen eating his dogs.

Shackleton's ship crushed

by ice, months exposed: snow-thistled beards,

frost-black digits, teeth split open

by cold. *Why did you come?*

Behind each comfort, Death hides –

but here I'm in the shiv

of his stare and he

in mine

Northwest Passage

There are many things I do not know.

I do not know why it took Moses and the Israelites

forty years to traverse a distance that could have been crossed

in eleven days. Perhaps twelve. A colleague told me this in indication

of how long it takes man to repent. This is another thing I know

nothing about. I only saw the journey of eleven days. Perhaps twelve.

I went to the library to review maps of Egypt to Canaan. The maps

were too recent to give any measurable sense of their journey,

and in any case Moses may not have had access to maps. I found

maps of the North Pole, both real and imagined. After months

of studying I still knew nothing about the North Pole. I read

about what one might eat, how one might wash, travel,

but still I knew nothing because I had not seen it. And so,

knowing nothing, I bought a boat and went.

★

The Arctic wanted to kill us. This was the first thing I knew.

The ice was not a substance but an organism, a Hydra, hell-bent

on chewing our sloop, Gjøa, to death. I clung to the bow for days.

Didn't eat. Didn't sleep. The wind's wheeled blades all but

skewered our souls out of our ribs. We overwintered with the Inuit,

trading tools for fox skins and lessons on building snow huts

and driving dogs. We learned their language, learned not to regard

ourselves in combat with the Arctic but symbiotic, weft in her

treachery, her stealth. This knowledge was wealth. Its application,

in thought and deed, brought about our late success.

Hammerfest Storm

Sea working its tools

       white hooks

shirring   wind

to a pelt   the ship akilter

a brute-thrown die   I crawl   starboard

wrap my body around a rail

to witness this quern

of land   grinding daylight

to better metal

Risøyhamn

At the kink of the strait
a mountain's garden
of homes:
daffodil, poppy-pink, cornflower.
We sail, snail-slow, beneath
a bridge knitting islands,
its grey echo
in the fjord
unstitched as we pass,
suturing in our wake.
O that all
rifts could be
so healed. O that these seas
never warm and rise but keep cool
wind prised between
bridge and tide.

Skarsvåg, Finnmark

Dog-loyal dark.

Boundaries between sky,

sea, and land don't apply

here. Fields of cirrus.

Bay an offcut

of exosphere. Fishermen

drape their haul – raw slivers

of moon – on hjell

to dry and salt, storing

remnants of light

The Queen Aboard the Oseberg

return her to that flame-
ocean beneath earth
to continue her journey –
but first, lay her in bed.
Prepare the best linens
and tuck her in, for she is
merely asleep, asleep
in dreams, rocked by death's
waves. Ready the sleighs,
the oxen, her dogs,
the stove, the plough. In this
new life she may
wish to reap and cook.
Leave nothing of use
behind. Seam the
helm in clay,
the dragon-
necked bow and stilled
oars, womb-tight.
Bury them all
and pray
a fair wind.

Light from the North

Ullr, god of winter, casts the *norðrljós,*

Bifröst, bridging heaven and earth,

but you may not know you've seen it.

Take this sleekit dark, cloud-scrubbed

save a curious ribbon of smoke-light

arching from one horizon to another: leave your

shutter open and smoke will skein

the black, moss-green and spectral. Or

risk the cold and wait – living flames,

night rainbow, might yet unspool,

bridging the distance home.

Troms Vigil

Mountain's thousand
flayed angles keep
vigil for our dying earth,
breaking her heart
each winter, all her old hurts
abstracting a ghost-
deep. Shroud-grim and watchful
mountain holds the ice
and though the seasons
are keening
and everything on earth
is ending
mountain's pale wings
may yet breach
hefting the Arctic
to true cold

The Story of Ice

Before film
there was ice
luring the relic
of a moment
into its press

before feathers and fur
there was ice
its shameless plumage
its down and pinion
its stupendous mane
and slap-cold fleece

before bricks and mortar
there was ice
hotels and cottages
crofts brochs tipis
yaodongs
fabulous ice yurts

before the rainbow
there was ice
its spectrum of aluminium
gold cerulean chartreuse even
blood

before the body
there was ice
venae cavae tunica
media alveolar aortic
femur
sacrum deltoid
twinkling astral womb

before desire
there was ice
crushing on every sunset
drinking in every cloud
holding on to each drop
of rain
like a love letter
or a kiss it wants to taste
again and again

before literature
there was ice
publishing wind's poems
ocean's gothic novels
flash fiction of the forests
memoir of an Ice Age
reprinted

before story
there was ice
earth's archive
museum of existence
in the first act there was ice
in the second act there was ice
and in the end there will be
ice

What We Found in the Arctic, or, the Geopolitics of New Natural Resources Uncovered by Melted Ice

Mme and M. Dumoulin, missing since 1942
Nickel
Rubber ducks
A Russian flag pronged on the seafloor
Copper
Three Incan children, sacrificed
Anthrax
Bird fossils from the Cretaceous period
Gold
Prehistoric skis
Saami, Nenets, Khanty, Evenk, Chukchi, Aleut, Yupik, Dolgan, and Inuit
Natural Gas
1700 species of plants
Record levels of microplastics
Diamonds
A hunter from 3000 B.C.
Oil
A horse from the Iron Age, with perfectly preserved manure
Territorial claims for the Arctic Continental Shelf
Polar bears, starving
Coal
Disputations concerning territorial waters
45,000 Russian troops
3,400 Russian military vehicles
41 Russian ships
15 Russian submarines
110 Russian planes
The albedo effect, claimed by no one

Where is the revolution?

Víkingar under Orion,
        Cygnus, scything

sheets of coal–dense sea
        through whipping rain

mile on mile. No
        shoulder of land

beyond dragonhead
        winking fire

in ship's belly
        honeying faces

fixed on home. Remember
        in these apocalyptic times

no tyranny or scourge
        defeated them –

when the old world
        broke, changed form

Víkings lifted oars
        and swords

            and became

                the storm

Trophic Asynchrony

this summery winter
    time doesn't want to be time any
more

conductor of the seasons'
ritornelle suited before meadows and love
ly
gardens raising her hands to prompt the poke
of crocuses   spiral of roses   the popping mush
rooms

time sets down her baton

language time [used to speak with history]
mistranslated as a text of daffodils
trumpeting in December   geese migrations clouding too
soon   uncreeping ice for penguins'
route home

time violently chucks her scales

balancing budburst with larvae unzippi
ng
from their crumb-
eggs to feed
  warmwaters for sea turtles   predat

ors arrivingin time to pic
k off pests
time for trees to shrugoff their green coats and r
est from nine
months' labour   creating breath
damping sound   sending rootparcels housi
ng insects animals huma

ns

everything hath a

    time has had enough ofbeinga mere *possess*
ion

27

a collision

pastpresentfuture

      today is a palimpsest of the Eocene
      reprising post-postmodern Paleozoic Paleo
cene
Holocene Juras
sic   realtime spacetime sidereal
cartography of progression repetition repeated

a bell tolls its own echo

how lucky we were

to be born in time

what will we do without her?

The Edge of the Known World

Seventy-one degrees north.

World's End. Nothing beyond this,

the Víkings knew it. They say

the English journeyed through Doggerland

to fish in Lofoten. I cannot imagine

how they managed the cold, the dark,

or what hunger drove them to survive

the cold and the dark. What hunger

will drive us yet, when I turn back

to the world of Brexit, nuclear arms,

Trump, islands of plastic, storms

beyond record? How will we measure

the cold? How will we see

in the dark?

Ode to a Tardigrade

This past month my timeline's
all apocalypse,
what with the calving
of the Larsen Sea Shelf,
the breeching of
the Doomsday vault, mass
extinctions, but today I
learned that you, O
moss piglet, micro
space bear, will out–
live the sun. Even
if a celestial event boiled
the oceans chances are
you'd stick around,
and if you got kicked
off the face of the
earth by, say, a giant
asteroid, you're fairly
capable of hanging
out in space. O tenacious phylum,
comma–armadillo, I
think of you kiting   to other
worlds   carrying some atomic
souvenir of us
      a song
      a germ
      a grain
as earth
chars to dust
again

II

We Have To Leave The Earth

He buried the letter in a forest near Auschwitz
where it hibernated for forty winters,
ampersands of his hand dormant
as field mice, and for all   he knew
the letter would never be found, snows
might drink the ink or the ground
swallow it as a grave. But
                              the urge to bear
witness moved him past consequence
of being found to speak of what   he said
to those he led to the gas chambers –
that they were not here to be bathed
as they'd   been told.
                    We are still in that place,
being moved past consequence or to death, or
to witness the taking of what is not owed.
We have not passed the urge to   obliterate
the Other. We have to leave the earth
because we know too many ways   to destroy
her, we have to write these things
we have to tell them to the forest
and the watchful snows.

There are always parts of a story that people forget

The war was over. She was four,
living with her grandmother.
Her father was jailed in Stalingrad
for feeding orphans. Her mother in Berlin,
sending money home. Russian soldiers
came on horseback.
Ten minutes to pack.

At gunpoint, the outcasts gathered
and walked. Twenty thousand
empty beds.

She woke in a morgue packed with bodies.
Their eyes fixed
on her.

At dawn, a colonel wanted her
as a gift for his wife.
The grandmother refused.
He cocked his gun.

In Austria, a refugee camp.
At eighteen, a husband in England.
Like those who have been split
and re-seamed in the mud-
knowledge of Being Other,
she kept walking
through countries of unbelonging.

Every night, in her mind,
the corpse-eye barrel of a gun
fixed on her.

Sagittarius A⋆

What makes a black hole the darkest chasm in the universe is the velocity
needed to escape its gravitational pull.
                    National Geographic, March 2014

You cannot see these holes, you only see what
                    they consume, unspooling electromagnetic

radiation from a celestial entity
                    like thread. Some say they don't exist.

Others say they are as old as the universe. What happens
                    inside is known by one in four people

at any given time. Still, the curvature of space
                    and the warping of time is difficult

to explain to a GP, or to friends who may
                    search for signs of physical injury.

You may be given an SSRI. You may try
                    and fail to develop a language

to explain the event horizon,
                    whereby all efforts to escape deepen the hole,

and speaking is often impossible.
                    You may physically contort, flip inside out,

be spaghettified, time travel, because
                    you've burned up an inner fuel. You

may arrive in another universe
                    where no mirror throws you back, and

even if you climb out the light that was ripped
                    from you might falter, a weighty cost.

But from one who fell in again and again
                    know it is never entirely lost.

Birdsong for a Breakdown

Because I'd swum a thousand miles in tar
upstream, and tar crept in my ears and ate the memory

of sound. Because I'd come to learn a new station
of madness, because I'd touched the soft seam of the self

and its infinite shadows. Because the material
revealed worlds on its B side, the side only seen

with eyes that are watchful for oblivion, and
because those worlds were so busy, and I wanted

to hear and know everything, everything, because
hope is not a human urge but the soul's last atom.

Because sweetness amidst such unnameable dark
is magnesium, too bright to miss, and so my ear

heard what I must have heard a thousand
times before and passed by without marvel – this time

my heart heard, too. That June, birdsong cleaved me
as rain splits drought, tonguing dry and bitter canyons,

quickening stooped flowers and knitting earth's cracks
which, in too much light, had yielded to rock. Heard with

those parts of me that had been burned to a new element
music revealing worlds in which birds were

not separate souls flitting between trees
but parts of me that could yet, even then, wing to joy.

Things Will Work Out

Things will work out.
Maybe not today, which has sadness
running through it like ore,
the mineral-tasting wind knocking cans
across the street and the disconsolate sea
banging its head off the desk.

You wonder where all the fog has come from.
Not the fog that creeps
in every September,
smudging the streetlights, but one
that's been made
from the scraps of your life.

The fears you believe in – *know* – are
coiling around your heart, your lungs,
building up a muscle
you don't realise you have. Somewhere
beyond here, a river is bending to velvety stones
along the bank, listening to their news.

On the hillside where you used to play
spears of emerald grass are folding
under the weight of rain. Jewel by jewel,
water passes to the earth, and the blades
straighten to sun again. A storm fritters
to breath. Traffic gathers. Things will work out.

Refinement

Hold me close, my chest is caving in
from the wrecking ball of guilt
that my narcissist made. She swung it from a long distance
and because I loved her I took it, blam,
square in the heart. All day I curled up
in a ball and took invisible blows from an invisible
baseball bat studded with nails. She said what happened
did not happen. She turned herself into a bomb
and detonated inside my brain. I no longer
know what is real or not real. Is this poem real?
Is this page real? Am I real? These are things she
makes me question. Her pain is greater
than mine. Her pain is a country, proof that she loved me
more than anyone, and the stadium of her pain is also proof
that I hurt her more than anyone else. I am inherently evil.
These are the beliefs I unpick from my skin every hour
like tiny hooks. If I appear to be distracted
it is because I am trying to survive
despite the thoughts that tell me I ought not to.
Each hook takes chunks of my soul
but I am persuaded that I will be better
once refined.

Peeling the Skin

They'd try to find the hem first,
the beginning of that lace-fine calyx that
sometimes ran deliciously
from shoulder to waist in a continuum
of cells shucked by too long
in the burning glare. No one thought to rub
in sun cream, it seems, for each summer
my lunar Irish epidermis crisped
from salmon to magenta before flaking
off great silvery coats and blankets,
milky curtains, pearl bodices.
The confetti of my childhood lies in corners
of Connemara, the sands of
Donegal, bearing traces of fingers
that picked me to riddance. I'd hear
the sellotape-tear
of strips they'd peel from my back
and I felt like something being primed for the spit,
or dressed for the rite. Sometimes
they'd shear
what wasn't ready for shearing, and blood would globe
at the new rind that knitted under the husk.
I think it was this small breach, this
being pared in pain
for others' pleasure, that taught me where DNA ended and
I
                    begin, and begin, and begin.

Erasing the Petroglyphs

After
the diagnosis

I retraced my steps

to the cave
where my wishes

for her future

were symbolically sung
in rock

I scraped

the blade
across each abrading

until the stone

was unsewn
newly hewn

and pause

in the earth-dark

for glyphs
to emerge

not of my hand

Pool

You tell yourself that the facts are clear:
autism is caused by genetics, or environment, and
even if you were to travel back in time you
could not have done anything, anything
at all to prevent this – you
think of her as a baby so often these
days, you envelop yourself in the before-
ness, in the sweetness of those early months – O
to hold her again in two palms running lengthwise along her body. O
to have the first seconds of her again
in your arms
in the bloodied birthing pool, slick, anchored to you
by a sky-blue rope, eyes sealed
shut. You slop through images
for signature, and the urge to pin the cause
on yourself, the one thing you can
touch, blame, wound,
is Viking strong. You ache to go
back to that pool, to the moment where she came
swift as a song, you want to lean into
echoes
grasp autism's root
which runs through your fingers
like red water –

Line Up

They said she had repetitive behaviours and that was the deal-breaker, the peak of the triad, the irrevocable sign of something more than a speech disorder, and because of this I didn't believe it, not fully. I nodded and said OK because they are the experts, and who am I but her mother, a witness, I cannot be objective precisely because I know her inside out, I cannot distinguish her from this condition that apparently seeped into her genes as the cells cusped and fluted the beautiful brain and the poppy-seed heart which we saw flickering on the screen at eight weeks, a white SOS on a wild dark island. O hazelnut, O hopeful beginning – today I watched her line up the water bottles again and again and again just to knock them down, and with each one all the hope I held back in the diagnostic meeting fell

down

down

down

At Sports Day

I watch her on the astro-turf
fringed by parents holding coffee cups
and agitated toddlers while the other Year
Ones file out in their colour-coordinated T-
shirts. She scans
the crowd and I wave
like I'm drowning
and when she spots me
her face lights up. *Mummy! Mummy!*
she says, bouncing on the spot.
Each time she finishes a race – egg on spoon,
pass the baton – there's that same look
back to check I saw, and when I
cheer she drinks it up. I swear
this to-and-fro smiling-and-cheering
is a kind of gold liquid
that floods those tender
parts of her rooting in the
earth of her being,
braiding her DNA, her subconscious,
forming the strength she'll draw on
thirty, forty, fifty years from now, here
in this small field by the school. I write
this down in case I forget, in case I forget
the gravity of these
too-quick gestures that are moon-
light frail but are ropes
tethering us, the kind that help us
not break in this hard world,
the kind that help us bear it out.

Willow's Leelo & Dave

The fish is blue and invisible.
His name is Leelo.
Leelo has backstory – his parents
are missing and he has to find them.
Until then, our daughter is looking after him.
He lives in a bowl filled with water.
The bowl is also invisible
and mostly she carries it around in
cupped hands, and at night she'll set it
beside the bed. We try to trick her
by asking 'where's Leelo?' and she
always remembers where
she left him. When she eats
or plays she gives Leelo to us for safe-
keeping. Luckily his bowl fits
in a trouser pocket, though she'll check
to make sure the bowl is all the way inside.
At school she's started a craze
for imaginary fish. All her friends suddenly
have imaginary fish. This time last year
the paediatrician said Willow didn't engage
in imaginary play, and this was a key reason
for her diagnosis. Now Leelo has
a friend called Dave, another fish.
He has backstory.
We help her carry them around.

Silent Things Speak to Me

As a child the inanimate and mute
would confess to me their moods, mostly
unbidden, though after a while

I thirsted for explanation. I
heard a cobweb trill the many names
for Irish wind

and once a doll in a shop window
whispered
that she was me. My father used his fist

to punctuate the danger
of hearing things. Now mother-
hood has turned my ear

inside out, tuned it to the pitch
of a chorus of ancestors,
women I've never met

but whom I often echo,
which has me thinking:
is even blood a translation?

Listen:

here come the children,

quiet to the bone
with their whole
bright selves.

Little Hand

sprout of light–
ammonite
my forefinger
this holding
go to sleep
through cot bars
as I can
she needs to
or perhaps she knows
and she
out of

made-flesh
around
always
on at bedtime
my arm stretched
as far
reach
know I'm there
I can't let go
holds on
mercy

My Father Shows Me His Knuckles

We sit on the side of the bed.
I ask to see his hands,
as though last night

was not of his making.
His right is the worst,
knuckles like red craters,

skin split and rolled
from where he punched the door
until the egg-box guts spilled out.

Godzilla on the black
and white TV on the nightstand.
Downstairs, limbless chairs

and the air a shout.
I cradle his hand,
read the storm

that blows all the way
from his childhood.
A voice inside his mind

tells him
someone else
did this to his hand.

1 day old, 6.03am

Let us stay beneath the covers and hold each other close while the dark taps its foot by the bedside, while the rain knocks at the window, pleading to come in. When you blow out seven candles the oceans will swell and all the polar bears will be gone. When you are twenty, one hundred and fifty million of us will have no homes. There will be no towns, no schools, no warm beds in which to hold each other in the still sure light. We will leave this planet for another, ascending into the billion galaxies ribboning above, the blue earth wrapped in a blanket we made, its million tears and frays in need of mending. I have brought you to a world riven by consequence. Let us remain in this small place a while longer. Push back the unknown night that waits, wanting to come in.

III

The House of Rest

A history in nine poems of Josephine Butler (1828–1906), who pioneered feminist activism, influenced key women's rights movements, such as the Suffragettes' movement, and successfully repealed the Contagious Diseases Act 1869, which facilitated sexual violence in the name of disease prevention.

Eva

Then you were here
real as a wound.

They placed you in my arms
with such care I thought you a parcel of feathers

that might fly away.
I stroked your face –

your eyes were midnight blue.
Time bended to you,

language re-strung its instruments
to sound your name.

Visitors admired your lace-
ears, your peony fists, but they

could not see you as I did –
you slid from your skin

just as you had slipped out of me
and became a shard

of morning light, turning
cobwebs to crystal thread,

the windowsill a gold bar,
dew on hedges constellations

of delicacy. I knew then
this love was alchemy.

Our bond is not made of that loose
wet rope they cut

but of instruments that show
the unseen and sound the silent,

the heart's infinite missions
harnessed in flight.

The Telling

Lord, I told Charles this morning about Eva.

Lord, is there anything in this world worse than a boy of seven
watching his beloved sister, his almost-twin, fall
to her death during a game, and learning that she died?

Lord, his beautiful face was the face of an old man's,
still as a saint's, emptied of childhood.

Lord, I pleaded for you to fill my mouth with words to heal
his silence, and I held him tightly and promised him
that You were holding his sister just so.

Lord, he asked if there were games in Heaven.

Lord, I thought on this and told him yes, there would be games
in Heaven.

Lord, Charlie asked if Eva would be fine during the games in Heaven
or if she would fall as she had fallen yesterday, and the terrible
shriek that had pierced me rang again in my ears.

Lord, I told him that she would never fall again
but was in Your arms. He quietened at this,
looked away, and asked in a voice that wrings my soul:
How could He have let her fall?

Lord, as Thou wilt: answer him.

Speak, Love

The casket was the length of her crib

white-washed oak with brass handles

What small offerings we make
to the things we cannot keep
as though we might bid them stay
a little longer, or fool ourselves

that love and time can be   tethered

When the men stood

      at either side
of the grave and lowered her

into the dark mouth
of earth

I shut my eyes tight   forced myself
to feel George's hand in mine

to know – to *know* – that she is not there
in the dark
but cradled in God's arms. I know

                  I know
we will see her again

but her absence is a mouth which holds me
between fear's teeth
      longing
for just one word
to be whispered

one word
    in her voice

Somnambulist

But I was in the dark, as I am
in the dawn and seed and the fawn-

soft mist that clings to roses,
a pretence of skin – a grief

at once vicarious and for myself.
I can undo neither. I fall

through the days, weeks,
months without her, my body

must learn different ways
of moving around the thousand

chasms of loss.
I do not sleep

but wake and wake and wake

Liverpool, 25th February 1866

Watercolour skies
above rain-oiled roads
and the back streets
which are fields, clotted with human waste
so thick you could grow potatoes.
My gaze turns from the ladies
on the silver pavements
shuffling like parasols, the men in their shadow-
black suits and tall hats, the carriages
that rattle like bags of coins
to those fields in the margins
of commerce, concealed
from the steamers at the docks.
You would not believe
that children are born there,
that lives are in the making
and unmaking – every day
the cholera carts
wheel in empty and wheel
out heaped, the only time
the children are counted
as treasure.

Picking Oakum

The matron shoves me into one of the ramshackle huts
        outwith the workhouse,
her hands trembling as she turns the key in the lock.

I expect to find a pride of lions inside, or perhaps wolves,
        but the hollow eyes watching
me belong to women – filthy, yes, filmed in soot and lice

and sadness, but women nonetheless, a dozen clasped
        by the foul shed with only two windows,
a leaky roof, and reams of old rope coiled on the floor

like black serpents. My hands are clasped, I know not
        where to sit, but at last I make do with the spot
on the floor that's haloed by thin noon-light, fanning out

my dress and sitting lower than my audience – this causes
        murmurs, which I ignore. *Now,* I say,
as brightly as I can muster, *who will show me what to do?*

An old woman gestures, a loop of rope already in both
        hands. *You pick it, ma'am. Take all the fibres apart.*
Like this, see? She pulls the strands, adds them to the cloud

by her feet. The women stir when I mimic the action,
        observing that my hands were not made
for this work, that I'd best not ruin my fingers or I'll

be sneered at by friends. *Not friends at all if they mock me,* I joke,
        and gradually the mood of the room
and the strangeness of the task is lightened by laughter. This

is how they cope, I think, for there is sisterhood
        in this terrible prison, palpable as the
wet brick walls and skittering rats. *What brought you here?*

a pregnant girl asks, and I say that I want to help them
        in any way I can, even if only to assist
in reaching their daily four-pounds of oakum required

by the matron. But then my mind floods with Eva, each
           woman's face a palimpsest of hers in reefs
of shade, and the true purpose of my visit unfolds: if born

under a different star my daughter might have found her way
           into this shed, into these lives, these pathways,
these tendrils of too-used rope. I tell them about her,

and I say that I undo this rope because I cannot undo her death,
           as I will undo all injustices that are within my reach.
And we are all crying and silent, and I pick the umbilical

shape in my lap
           as though this black rope might lead me
back to her, as though I'll find her at the end.

The Women in My Bed

I am no suffragist
but a womanist, and if there is anything
I cannot abide it is the selling
of virtue for tuppence, and if there
is anything I abhor it is the selling
of virtue for tuppence else a woman will die
of hunger, and if not hunger, she will die
of cold in the street, her feet bare,
her soul too heavy for her body.

       So they are here: five *destitutes* under our roof,
       five *incurables*, as we explained to Cat,
       Henry and Charlie. Our friends think me
       mad and George even madder
       for permitting it. *It is obscene! Five*
       prostitutes! They are girls, I replied,
       children of God, and they are dying.
       An acquaintance of George refused to cross
       our threshold in protest. *Where are they?* he
       demanded, and
       I could not help
       myself. I said,
       upstairs, I should imagine,
       asleep in my bed.

The irrepressible flicker of zeal before
he turned on his heel.

The House of Rest

Matthew 11: 28

George and I have found a second house
to rent at two-hundred-and-fifty pounds a year –
for this we shall provide a home for thirteen women.
I wish it could accommodate more, but for now
we shall make a little heaven
for those *stained and dying Magdalenes* to live
in comfort, to come to know their God
before they meet Him.

       Their time is short, despite
our doctor offering his services *pro bono*.
He can but bring relief of pain
as they bear out their day. Remarkable that
Eliza, the youngest, counts herself fortunate to die
in such a place! *So many others have to take men
even while they're dying,* she says. *How it must
harrow them to die with such indignity!*

       Her words
have drilled through me all the day long. Our
House of Incurables puts us all at great risk
of harm by those folk who consider us to be furthering the cause
of prostitution (perish the thought!) I have been
spat at, called a villain and a whore, and yet
my mind will not be turned: I must do more.

The Quiet Girls

In Chatham I spent one whole night
in going into the brothels of the town.
You would have thought it was a Mayan
ritual of human sacrifice, or the Danaïdes

choosing husbands who knew they'd
be killed, such was the air of reluctance
on the part of the soldiers, some just thirteen,
and the *girls wearing tickets*. For this

children and women are forcibly subjected
to a brutal examination – bound, gagged, feet
in stirrups, metal speculum – in the name of
controlling venereal disease. Many have died;

all carry the trauma throughout their days.
They are detained at lock hospitals
for up to a year, and often a parson is present,
permitting this *indecent assault* upon her person.

Said one to me, *"I am not a woman; I am*
simply a tool." Reducing one with *a Divine right*
to protect the secrets of her own person to chattel
is to steal her identity, her humanity,

her voice. These Acts debase the most
vulnerable of society, silence the weak,
protect brute men at the cost of quiet girls,
thus when I demand that you repeal this law

I speak for the womanhood of the world.

IV

Listen

to the smallness of water
                    in its brief cauldron –

to the laugh of rain
                    in its flawed wound –

to the voice that
                    noses all your sore spots

in its terrific flamingo
                    that sutures echo to echo

Sweet Pea

I

It would have been easy to tear
the tendrils that choked them,
keeping the whole bunch bowed
in a bramble
instead of arcing up to light –
I took my daughter's hand,
showed her the fine threads
coiled tight in desperation,
and I thought of the ultrasound,
how we had to root in the shadows
for an echo of bones.
Arms up, her ghost-hands spread
before the torchlight of the Doppler
like a hold-up. When she was born
the indigo twine of the cord
was twisted so tight
I thought it might snap back
when they cut it, and as if thinking the same
she felt for my finger, holding on tight
as they divided us
into our equal parts.

II

I could not tear them, though
she urged me to quit my careful
unlooping of noose-fibres
and compromise with a break here,
a rip there, loosening most of them to sun
at the cost of a damaged few.
She grew bored, went inside, returned
with a stool so I could rest
my knees while maintaining the task
of what must have resembled lassos
in the air. I wanted to explain
that I had never seen anything as pure
as the two-second-old creature
thickened with wax and blood
settled into my arms, a human
optic through which the world
began to filter. She was yet
too young to understand and took
my efforts to save a bunch of small
stems as stubbornness. I can't
be sure, but when the first white
purse opened I saw her measure
persistence against force,
an inner weather.

Thwaites

I thought flipping the boats would wake you up
bleached reefs in palliative care
trees sparking leaves of flame
hills buckling to mud
tide scratching out a city I thought
blue whales full of trash
dolphin calves poisoned by mothers' milk
and all those plastic full-stops guttering like fish
eggs in the bowels of the Mariana Trench would
shake you into a rethink but man if
hurricanes balled up in twelve hours
don't make you sit up and see what's happening
imma tell you there's a hole in me
yup where my belly used to be
enough to lift the seas ten feet
if you don't drown you're a refugee
if you're not a refugee you'll be bombing them
if you're not bombing you'll be eating them
if you're not eating you'll be fighting
off plague and climbing on the last boat
I'll ever flip

Homeschooling

I'm teaching my children what's happening
right now, which is to say I'm dredging
an ocean of oil-black sludge into our home.
So foul it makes us retch, I'm hauling into
their minds centuries of humans
on their knees, gagged, raped, chained.

Do I want to tell them their home is built
on blood and bones? Do I want their
childhood garden filled with teargas,
Mace, a knee on the neck? The fact is,
sludge is already bubbling up the plug holes,
dripping off the roof, gunking our pipes
as we sit down to dinner, faced with
starvation or a feast of diseased flesh.

Hawking Radiation

Haul out.
The universe is being gutted
four billion years after

we let the ice caps powder –
        so pile up the neuron stars
        like old office chairs.

You there! Up-end the supergiants ready
for the grinder. Tear down Andromeda,
wipe out the equations and graphs

chalked up by a keen hand.
Don't pine for the collapsing prisons
of matter –

all things, even sorrow,
        so soon run
        out their rent.

Hymn to be Sung Underwater

Earth, our mother,
life-giver, not *home*

but host,
protector,

archangel,
nurturer of eye,

soul, lungs,
the mercurial

human heart –
each structure of life

calls you:
ovum, womb,

nucleus, cell.
Both tomb

and spring,
old love,

last port,
faithful vessel,

forgive our short
shrift,

O finite
gift.

The Sky Beneath Our Feet

'Anaximandros of Miletos, son of Praxiades, says that the first principle of things is the infinite; for from this all things come, and all things perish and return to this.'

Aetius, *Doxography* (Plac. i. 3: Dox. 277), late 1st century BC

What he saw: fish laid out on stalls
at the marketplace, arrowhead pattern of scales
repeated in the nets that caught them,
shadows sliced on the gnomon's tongue
for time's sake. What he did not see
was the earth from space: a child's blue
and white marble tossed into black.
Yet, like fish drowned in air

to sustain different breath, he knew sky
loops beyond night in boundless re-beginning

or, in other words, he saw without sight.

Notes

p. 33, *There are always parts of a story that people forget* – I am referring here to the Brno Death March of 30 May 1945, when thousands of ethnic Germans, including my grandmother-in-law, were expelled from Brno to Austria. Those that survived lived in refugee camps for years afterwards.

p. 34, *Sagittarius A★* - Sagittarius A★ is the name of our galaxy's supermassive black hole, situated in the middle of the Milky Way galaxy. It weighs the equivalent of about 4 million suns.

p. 37, *Refinement* – I was thinking here about Hannah Arendt's statement in *The Origins of Totalitarianism*, where she declares that 'The ideal subject of totalitarian rule is... people for whom the distinction between fact and fiction (i.e., the reality of experience) and the distinction between true and false (i.e., the standards of thought) no longer exist.'

p. 15, *Northwest Passage* – Norwegian explorer Roald Amundsen was the first person to successfully navigate the Northwest Passage, the route across the Arctic linking the Atlantic and Pacific Oceans. Amundsen's boat, the *Gjøa*, was just 21 metres long – a larger ship would never have made it through the ice at that time – carrying a crew of just six men. Amundsen's successful journey (from 1903-1905), his relationship with the Inuit, and his scientific findings made a major contribution to polar ethnography and knowledge of the magnetic north pole.

p. 20, *The Queen Aboard the Oseberg* – the Viking Museum in Oslo holds the Oseberg ship, discovered in an Oseberg burial chamber in 1903 and containing two women, one of which was Queen Åsa Haraldsdotter. In 834 AD, the ship was buried in blue clay – a fitting vessel to ferry the Queen to the afterlife.

p. 25, *What We Found in the Arctic, or, the Geopolitics of New Natural Resources Uncovered by Melted Arctic Ice* – the albedo effect relates to the reflection of light off a surface. In this context, light reflecting off the snow-covered (white) surfaces of the Arctic is crucial because it bounces light back to the sun and keeps the area cool. The less ice, the more sunlight (and thus heat) is absorbed by the water, thus speeding up the warming of the sea. With thanks to https://secretsoftheice.com, and https://www.vox.com/a/borders/the-arctic for information relating to Russian's military presence in the Arctic.

p. 49, *The House of Rest* – following the untimely death of her little girl during a game of play in the family home, Josephine Butler (1828-1906) threw herself into overturning the Contagious Diseases Act of 1869, which allowed any girl over the age of 13 to be forcibly subjected to a horrific medical examination of her cervix, and interned for up to a year, on mere suspicion of possessing venereal disease. Butler's campaigns came at great personal cost, and she routinely befriended prostitutes and invited them to live with her. Despite her work and enormous influence, however, Butler's name has largely been erased by history, like so many other female pioneers. Some works of scholarship provide essential reading on Butler. See, for example, Jane Jordan, *Josephine Butler* (John Murray, 2001) and, for further context on the Victorian period, Kelly Lynn Trumble, *"Her Body Is Her Own": Victorian Feminists, Sexual Violence, and Political Subjectivity*, PhD Thesis, 2004, Florida State University. Italicised lines from 'The Quiet Girls' (p. 59) are taken from the minutes of Butler's examinations by the Select Committee on Contagious Diseases Act in May 1882. These are archived at the Glasgow Women's Library. Other poems feature lines from a variety of Butler's letters, which are archived at the Women's Library in London.

p. 65, *Thwaites* – Thwaites glacier is an enormous ice shelf that is currently melting at an unprecedented rate into the Antarctic. Thwaites acts as a keystone, holding the ice sheet together, thus its collapse will likely trigger the rapid collapse of many other glaciers, with resulting global catastrophe 'next to a meteor strike'.

p. 67, *Hawking Radiation* – in 1974 Stephen Hawking theorized that black holes – one of the most destructive and energetic forces in the universe – are dying from an unknown form of radiation, and that the universe too will die.

Acknowledgements

Thanks are due to the editors of those publications where drafts of these poems first appeared: *Literary Hub, The Poetry Review, The Stinging Fly, The Compass Magazine, From Glasgow to Saturn, Ambit, And Other Poems, The Interpreter's House, The Northern Poetry Library Anthology, New Welsh Review, Butcher's Dog, Witches, Warriors, Workers: An anthology of contemporary working women's poetry.* Thanks also to my wonderfully supportive colleagues at the University of Glasgow: Zoë Strachan, Louise Welsh, Colin Herd, Sophie Collins, Elizabeth Reeder, and especially Jen Hadfield. Thanks to Ruth Stacey, Kathryn Maris, Angela Smith, Amy Wack, and all at Seren.

'My Father Shows Me His Knuckles' was shortlisted for the *London Magazine* Poetry Prize in 2016. 'Sagittarius A*' was a finalist in the Aesthetica Creative Writing Competition 2017. 'The Sky Beneath Our Feet' was commissioned by the Northern Poetry Library for its 50th anniversary. *The House of Rest* was exhibited at Woodhorn Museum & Northumberland Archives and Palace Green Library, Durham throughout July 2016 and January 2017. 'Homeschooling' was included in the *Best Scottish Poems* 2020 Anthology by the Scottish Poetry Library, edited by Janette Ayachi.